Poetry Written While Walking Dogs

November 2019 – June 2021

Alex Lazarus-Klein

Poetry Written While Walking Dogs

Copyright 2021 by Alex Lazarus-Klein

All Rights Reserved

ISBN: 978-1-257-83108-1

Dedicated to my official pandemic team: Ashirah, Jarah, Boaz, Noam and our two pups, Akiva and Nava.

Contents

Preface 5
   "Small Moments Make a Big Impact on our Days." 6

PRE-COVID 9
   My daughter 10
   Humans 11
   Gravity 12
   The Very Thing That Makes us Fly 13

Early Covid 15
   What it's like right now 16
   Frozen in Time 17
   After the Death of George Floyd 18
   The cell 19
   The line 20
   To The Supreme Creator 23

Later Covid 25
   Canadice Lake 26
   Nostalgia 27
   Bird Song 289
   Post Election Hues 31
   Lake Erie in Winter 33
   Akron Falls 35
   Incandescent Spaces 36
   From the Perspective of a Tree 38

Post Covid 39

Poetry Written While Walking Dogs

Return to Normal 40

The Fox 41

Her Last Concerto………………………………………………..42

Waltzing Down Maple 43

Poetry Written While Walking Dogs

Preface

What better time to write poetry than in long early morning walks with my pups during a pandemic? Finding time to jot down a few notes and shape a poem has helped me cope during these difficult times. I am blessed to have a loving family, a safe home, and a stable job. I hope you too find humor, happiness, and a sense of the divine in these musings.

Poetry Written While Walking Dogs

Buffalo News, My View Column, Published April 2, 2021, Alex Lazarus-Klein

"Small Moments Make a Big Impact on our Days."

Our two sets of dogs - my brown mutts, one an Australian Herder and the other a Boxer mix, and their black curly haired poodles - have crossed paths countless times over the past year. As we weave around the quiet streets of Eggertsville, it has come to the point that we almost expect to see one another on our morning rounds - the dogs staring wide eyed at one another, tongues and tails wagging, trying to get their owners to stop to pay a visit..

The other couple and I do not actually know one another. As we try to manage our dogs, there is little time for actual conversation. And, yet, our lives through our shared activity are somehow intertwined. Each of us among the millions of global citizens who adopted canines during the pandemic. Like kayaking and bicycling, raising pets has been a useful distraction in such chaotic and confusing times.

Walking my dogs has been cathartic. It is the one time I get a little fresh air, and a break from the endless hours on Zoom. It is also the time when I will often check in with my synagogue president, trying to make sense of the constantly changing guidelines. Last March, it was on one of these walks that we made the fateful decision to shut down all in-person activities, and it is also where we talked a year later about our reopening plans.

Every morning at approximately seven, I begin my journey, weaving past my *cul de sac*, around the adjacent parks and side streets for several miles, until eventually returning home. Along the way I witness a unique snapshot of suburban life. In addition to the poodles, there are pugs, Labradors, and golden retrievers. By now, I know their

Poetry Written While Walking Dogs

individual homes and owners. We know one another's routes, tactfully crossing the street to avoid direct contact with one another.

There are also the runners, bursting out with water bottles in hand, or dripping with sweat on their return home. A Methodist minister around the corner from me who participates in off-road marathons, has been taking his ten-year-old daughter out for part of his run. The two of them run side by side like seasoned partners. My next door neighbor chugs along at a jogger's pace, trying to recover from leg injuries he suffered the year before. Lately, he has been increasing his pace as he gains confidence in his conditioning.

Wednesday is trash day, and the large blue recycling and garbage trucks methodically move from receptacle to receptacle, gracefully maneuvering their mechanical arms to dispose of the waste. These brave essential workers have become heroes for their persistence during the worst of the pandemic. I flash a thumbs up sign as I pass them, my dogs excited by the commotion.

I often run into a congregant who is an infectious disease specialist. He walks his granddog, a small brown spaniel, right past my street. He gives me an inside scoop on how the fight against Covid-19 is developing. Lately, he has been increasingly more optimistic. "It will all start clearing up in the summer," he assures me.

Over the course of the year, these walks have moved from tense affairs where I was petrified to even dispose of doggy bags, to easy jaunts oddly removed from this time period altogether. Along the way, the younger of my pups, Nava, has grown from a tiny spark plug, to a muscled one-year-old. My dogs, as well as the poodles for the other couple, have become beloved family members. Our walks together will hopefully continue long after the pandemic is over.

Poetry Written While Walking Dogs

Poetry Written While Walking Dogs

PRE-COVID

My Daughter

she turned like
Lot's wife turned
to see Sodom and Gomorrah destroyed

like Sisyphus turned
to see the boulder roll
down the hill

like Orpah turned
to see Ruth and Naomi
disappear from view

she turned back to me
to check if I was still there
The bus toward middle school

seemed so far away
I was the dutiful father
watching as she boarded

watching as it pulled away
now it was my turn to turn
the bus receding from view

my heart like salt
turned statuesque
like boulder rolled away
like Orpah was turning to return home

Humans

we are restless creatures
unable to sit like kings over the plains of the Sahara

we who are startled by shadows
even when we do fly refuse to soar

it is not in our nature
a cockroach can remain still far longer

we may admire the owl's keen eyesight
but we cannot duplicate her stare

we simply have no patience for waiting
how frantic we must look, darting

on ambiguous path, despairing of the journey
even when the only one chasing us is ourselves

Gravity

remove your socks
pluck the lint from between your toes
shake off all excess skin
and still you will be standing on something

deprive the earth of all of its air
hurl yourself unto outer space
take off your very appendixes
and still you will be standing on something

better to just accept and embrace
the feeling of curled feet
of pinched nerves
of gravity itself

when you are ready take time
to thank the dust
pay homage to spirits
shout out your grievances to the Gods

then slightly freer
hang upside down
allowing the hair on your head
to float like tentacles

focus on the tips of hair at their ends
feeling the pressure ever so slightly
of someone else
whose feet are resting upon yours

The Very Thing That Makes Us Fly

There is so much sadness
oceans of it—
whole planets.

If we are not watchful
it can seep into
our every moment

and round them like a tear.
If you haven't already
watch for it—

on the faces of those you love
(even the happiest among us).
Listen to it in song and story

in the very air we breathe.
You ask for me to cry with you
and not stand up and walk away.

So much of it seeps into me
like oceans, planets,
like your soul itself.

Hoping that the deep black hole
you say sits in your dreams
will lift off your heart

flying like a shadow
and disappear into the darkness
of the room in which we sit.

Sadness is just that
(feel it even in this poem)
the very thing that makes us fly.

Poetry Written While Walking Dogs

Early Covid

What It's Like Right Now

Yes, the crows still feasted on a plastic cup.
Yes, my dog still sniffed the grass for hidden rabbit poop.

Yes, a family of does still stood hesitantly munching grass.
Yes, I still had to look both ways when crossing between Longmeadow and Ivyhurst.
And, yet, something was different.

The fragile shell of the sky seemed to encroach a little closer to the earth.
My heart leapt a little higher when encountering a passerby.
And I felt a little less fine in returning home.

There are moments while lying alone in my room
a gentle light filtering in through the shades
I can close my eyes and pretend.

But, even then, I can sense a difference like a thin veil of sour air.
Harken weary travelers, take hold of what you love -
let it seep into you like water absorbed in a bath,
learning to pair how you want things to be with how they in fact are.

Frozen in Time

standing still I imagined
the earthworms
never venturing past the small
swath of land they inhabit

or the trees feeling all manner of life
grazing on their exteriors and not being
able to do a single thing about it
we watch our surroundings to see what is moving

we notice the grass rustling in the wind
a squirrel scurrying in the yard
the sparrows circling overhead
but these things are unusual

very little in life moves at all
I am comforted by this thought
knowing that nothing I could do
or that anyone else could do to me

while I am still living
and breathing in this world
would ever allow me to stand still
in one place for very long

After the Death of George Floyd

I come to you without benefit
of sight or sound

in absence of cultural motif
or geographic pin

you do not know my God
nor that of my ancestors

I have removed all imprint
of the human condition

still I fear
you see only my exterior

the loose fitting body I inhabit
the subtle shift of my eyes

assumptions you have
about who I am and how my life should be

but what if I could truly erase those from your mind
cleanse them from your experience

could you sit still in what you might never know
could you be present without fear or presumption

or would you like many others before you walk away
fearing nakedness might be contagious

and after all is said and done
we may not be quite as different
as you initially perceived

The Cell

the cell
as soon as it is born
begins to decay

the sun has only a
certain amount of time
making its rounds in the sky

even the tiny dots
millions of light years from us
will one day extinguish

as the physicists remind us
entropy will envelop us all

I wake up make my bed
put one foot before another

knowing each step is one less
I will take and still I step
cells aligned bones firm

pressed against earth
that even as we speak
floats gently away

The Line

the line
I drew
with pen
and ruler
careful not to
smudge
the edges
perfectly
straight
without indentation
or abbreviation
exactly as I
had intended
until closer
inspection revealed
a minute break
an upturn
and a downturn
a slight wave
missed
at first
but clearly present
so I erased
and started
over
this time
no mistakes
perfect
a line

no one could
cross
not even I
my resolve
too strong
impenetrable
but even
as I contemplated
the process
brought pen and ruler
to paper
I realized
there was
no point
All lines
are just
collections
of dots
none strong
enough to withstand
the frailty of
the human
heart

Poetry Written While Walking Dogs

To the Supreme Creator

the wind was ripping through the trees
as it tends to where I live

I sat on a hot dry day
below the gentle pines in my backyard

enjoying the energy of it all
knowing that some days

I may sit stoic and inconsequential
or choose not to rise at all

still despite my best attempts
the world will give a vigorous response

tormenting the landscape
destroying my meager garden

or maybe even tossing a few
loose shingles

and I as is my right
can simply allow that energy beyond me to envelop me

without the slightest need
to even move into the shade

ultimately be reliant
on forces much beyond my own design

I am somehow comforted resting weary one leg upon another
in a fashion my wife tells me is bad for my back and feeling pride

that just a tiny speck of creative matter could be deserving of
such immense demonstrations of supreme power and love

Poetry Written While Walking Dogs

Later Covid

Canadice Lake

we lay on the lake today like glass
below us the turtle grass poked through
as the shadow of clouds hid the sun

on the mountain side pine trees lapped against the slight breeze
I asked my older daughter
how she might draw them

my youngest son closed his eyes as I pushed the oars of our kayak
we had taken off our masks
because no one was around

For hours we circled until we were too far from shore
to just be pushed back by the current
when we emerged

the kayaks sat like colorful flowers by the side of the road
we drove like we were still swimming
the blue sky watery like a lake

Nostalgia

I went chasing after places
I've already been
sitting in pine groves

as the light
hit them
just so

remembering where
you once ran
on pudgy legs

up steep inclines
so proud you
made it to the top

you are chasing chickens
as I fend off
lurking roosters

I want to show you
my child
exactly how it felt

as we walk ahead
trampling over
freshly fallen leaves

but no matter how
hard I try

I can't

You stand so far away
(your legs not so
pudgy anymore)

too much has happened
you need your own
holding place

where memories can
blow like breeze
and you too

could hope
for so much more
than this world can offer

Bird Song

I never thought of the plight
of the birds in a storm

always afraid for my own safety
will the walls of my house hold

will the electricity go out
will the dogs ever stop their insufferable cries

my heart pulsates just a little stronger
as I hold tight to you

our tall pines bending back and forth
outside our window

I fear for them as well
but what about the creatures

who make homes in their limbs
who will protect them

do the squirrels simply scurry underground
and what about the starlings

is their sweet song stifled
or does it grow louder

rising with the gales
screaming out to the world
all will be okay

Post Election Hues

The morning after the election
everything seemed partisan,
even the trash receptacles bled blue.

my neighbor's red wooden lawn chairs-
already overturned for winter -
a beautiful shade of auburn.

The leaves of the Nandina bush
most definitely red.

Only a throng of leftover Halloween ghosts,
hanging from a birch,
refused to take sides.

Limp American flags,
folded over by the slight breeze,
felt depressingly like electoral maps.

Did I mention the red door
I encountered while walking my dogs -
already dressed in a Christmas wreath?

Then the sky over the baseball field
was streaked by long pink clouds
overlaying a beautiful tapestry of blue -

Betsy Ross would be proud.
I snapped a picture
just to remember the feeling

removing my boxer pup's red leash,
I sat down to eat my
blueberry yogurt in peace.

Lake Erie in Winter

The lake was not a lake,
but a vast expanse of snow -

a wilderness of deserted space.
And, aside from a few loose gull tracks, pristine,

filled with gorgeous bumps of frozen waves.
My children ran into it, dove,

swam in stillness with heavy black boots
and colorful reflective coats and gloves.

We had gone beyond the lake
found our way to an unknown planet.

Getting further and further from the shore,
a Tiki Bar stood distant, abandoned,

a reminder of the world we had left behind,
sullen without sand and sun.

We walked until the ice began to crack,
following our own tracks back,

occasionally falling into deep holes
which swallowed our legs,

laughing as we pulled one another out,
freezing, but giddy, climbing back into our car,
like a spaceship, ready to return home.

Poetry Written While Walking Dogs

Akron Falls

You insisted going one way
I the other
You were right

There were so many people
the kids kept dipping their feet
in the snow

on the side of the path
almost falling through
It was a disaster

then we turned the corner on a waterfall
frozen in place it left us gaping
sliding between the ice

we went behind
looking at the world differently
the kids no longer fighting

this is how winter should look
if it did
I would be here all the time

Incandescent Spaces

I would rather be like leaf tossed
from high tree limb of aged oak

meant to drop without balance
waffled by wind

tormented by gnarled branches and left to fend
in uproarious open space

than the beautiful tear dropped Japanese maple
whose red speckled yellow

glides gently like light itself
subsumed by loving ground

on landscape of neglect and abuse
to still look glorious under foot

do not lose yourself in the way things are
find the resilient cherish them

allow their spirits to fly off with the wind

Poetry Written While Walking Dogs

From the Perspective of a Tree

Trees do talk, but what are they saying?
 I scan the sparse outcrop lining our street –
which one should I consult?
Is that tree middle-aged or just fat?

The oak that forks in the center seems promising.
The roots of an elm clench like a person flexing.
This small sapling has bent arms
to avoid the electrical wires.

Looking up, I notice this is not a tree at all –
but a signal booth.
Do any of them have the faintest idea of
what existed before this *cul de sac*?

The soil is rich in bog.
I fantasize about renting an armchair
relaxing in the plot that will one day become a house.
My house.

Here - before Japanese maple was even a thing -
I will plant a forest.
The trees in my forest will actually bisect one another,
competing for sunlight.
No humans or their descendants allowed.

Poetry Written While Walking Dogs

Post Covid

Return to Normal

remember this time
when you looked at me
with premonition

like two army brigades we stood
on opposite sides of the street
you with your dog

I with mine
we looked stony-eyed at one another
what store of weapons were you carrying

we nodded in mild acquiescence
and then marched quietly
back to our own homes

scrubbing away any hint
of our interaction
remember this time

and do not be dismayed
for battles of this kind
are beyond our own comprehension

we are neighbors in the truest sense of the word
allied in our mutual cohabitation
of this ever tilting earth

that one day will have us holding one another
in celebration of all that we endured
in those uncertain days

The Fox

for some reason
I kept thinking of the fox
the way she stood staring
then ducked behind the tall grass
like an apparition

we were passing by at high speeds
the animal's head cocked sideways
a ball of light red fur
looking right at us
a fox I had pointed

sitting by our porch table later
sipping after dinner wine
as you gazed distractedly out ahead
focused intently on whatever it was
you were thinking

no a coyote you finally said
I stopped unsure of what you meant
then all at once I knew
you were thinking about my comment
funny how that moment had stayed with us

I looked down at our dogs
sprawled out on the grass relaxing
remembering the way coyotes hunted
feigning injury drawing dogs in
and then devouring their naive cousins

Poetry Written While Walking Dogs

my heart shuddered thinking back
had my initial impression been so wrong
could a coyote be that size
yes you replied
the whole day began unraveling

no longer a fox or a coyote
just an unknown animal staring
considering our car as we passed
before ducking into the grass
well past where either of us could see

Her Last Concerto

In-joy, she said, with a smile
About almost anything, her best friend said -
Even when she schlepped me off for hernia surgery
Always an emphasis on joy and not on the in.

We were standing by her graveside
laughing as she would have wanted.
She had asked us tell stories,
Only a few of us gathered in the veterans section

She has not served, as of such,
but loved taking her Alaskan Malamutes to the VA.
American flags waved slightly in the breeze.
Her daughters lounging on cemetery chairs.

Look up to the reams of light and song
she had written on a note to both of them
instructions for what to do after she died
Where no one says farewell

Was it really even goodbye?
Having accompanied her to the grave.
We tucked her into bed -
a violin playing in the background- in-joy!

Waltzing Down Maple

I know it was going to be ok
when the porch sales started reappearing -
long rows of wicker baskets and baby strollers,
mixed with colorful potted plants.

Golfers were out on the range
methodically slapping balls across the dry grass
I caught sight of an older woman
tilting down her mask to reveal her nostrils.

The hydrangeas were blooming and the kids
jaunted off the school bus like tiny insects.
I, too, wanted to revel, dancing across
supermarket aisles that months before

had seemed like dark alleyways -
Cheerios and Cap'n Crunch giving me the stink eye.
V Day had arrived. I wanted to be the sailor
who smooched the anonymous nurse.

Anything was possible, pandemic be damned,
nothing could prevent my mask less smile
from taking a long look in the rearview mirror,
naked except a slight hint of unkempt beard.

Poetry Written While Walking Dogs

Alex Lazarus-Klein came to Buffalo in the fall of 2008 to serve as the rabbi of Temple Sinai, now called Congregation Shir Shalom. He brings warmth, creativity, and compassion to the role of synagogue rabbi. A 2004 graduate of the Reconstructionist Rabbinical College he also holds Masters and Bachelor Degrees from the Jewish Theological Seminary, as well as a Bachelor's degree in creative writing from Columbia University. He currently resides in Amherst, with his wife Ashirah, three young children, Jarah, Boaz, and Noam, and two dogs, Akiva and Nava.

Made in the USA
Monee, IL
18 September 2021